Foreword

When planning to buy a pet, it is very important to gather plenty of information, even if it is only a small animal such as a rabbit. Does the pet fit into your family? How much work is day-to-day care and what will it cost to buy, house and keep? Is the animal happy to be cuddled, or does it prefer to be admired from a distance? This book offers an overview of the various rabbit breeds, their characteristics and their needs. It aims to be a guideline for responsible care, which includes various aspects of the rabbit's life. If you plan to breed rabbits, this book can lead you on your first steps in this gripping, versatile hobby.

This book is not a comprehensive reference book about rabbits. We could fill a whole book just with the different breeds, but you can find helpful basic information about rabbits here. What do you need to look out for when buying an animal, for example? How is a hutch built, and what does a rabbit eat? You can also find information on behaviour, shows, colourings and breeds, reproduction and your rabbit's health.

A rabbit is a pet that requires daily care. Do not go and buy a rabbit without further thought. Does a rabbit fit into your family? Are your children old enough to take (some) care of a rabbit? Have you got enough room for a rabbit? If you know what you are doing, a rabbit can be a pleasant companion, both for you and your children.

About Pets

the Rabbit

A guide to selection, care, housing,

nutrition, health and breeding

Contents

about pets

A Publication of About Pets.

Copyright © 2003
About Pets
co-publisher United Kingdom
Kingdom Books
PO9 5TL, England

ISBN 1852792175
First printing
September 2003
Second printing
April 2005

Original title: *het konijn*
© 2002 Welzo Media Productions bv,
About Pets bv,
Warffum, the Netherlands
http://www.aboutpets.info

Photos:
Rob Dekker, Dick Hamer,
Kingdom Press and Rob Doolaard

Printed in China through Printworks Int. Ltd.

In general

Rabbits have been kept as pets since Roman times. They were kept then for their tasty meat and their beautiful coat. Today, rabbits are still kept as farm animals, but most rabbits lead a more pleasant life as companions for humans.

Despite common belief, rabbits are not rodents. A rabbit belongs to the hare-family *(Lagomorpha)*. Research has shown that, anatomically speaking, rabbits have more in common with this order. Rabbits and other hare-family members have not two, but four incisors in the upper jaw. The domestic rabbit descends from the common European wild rabbit. The earliest ancestors of the rabbit and other *Lagomorphae* seem to have existed in the cretaceous period. It is suspected that they were insect eaters from the family of *Pseudictops*. These developed to a descendant that looked more like the hares and rabbits we know today.

The order of the hare-likes consists at the moment of approximately twenty types of hare, thirty types of rabbit and ten types of Pika (Rock Rabbit). Apart from the Pika, all varieties look similar. They also look very much like their ancestors, although they are spread over the whole world, and live in different climates.

Many sorts of animals have adapted to changes in climate and habitats. Hares and rabbits have not changed very much and they still show many primitive characteristics. It seems that these animals are capable of surviving almost anywhere without having to adapt. The hares have, however, like almost all animals in the wild, adapted to their environment with the colour of their coat. It is white in the snow, yellow-grey in the prairie and dark in the forests.

Hare family members are found almost anywhere in the world, from the North Pole to Australia. The only places where they are not to be found are the South Pole, Madagascar, parts of Indonesia and the southern part of South America. Wild hares generally have primitive brains, which means that they are not particularly intelligent. They compensate for this with highly developed hearing and an excellent sense of smell. Only a few varieties make noises. They vary in length and weight from twelve centimetres and one hundred grams to seventy centimetres and seven kilos.

Rodent Incisors

One of the very few things rodents and rabbits have in common are their rodent incisors. Rabbits, like rodents, have constantly growing incisors without roots. There are two in the upper and two in the lower jaw. These teeth are extremely strong, but do get worn down by their constant gnawing. Nature has found a solution: the teeth keep growing, the whole life long. There is, however, a disadvantage to this. If the upper and lower teeth no longer fit properly onto each other, due to a deformed jaw or a hard knock, they are no longer 'stopped' by the opposite tooth. They grow

Hare

unchecked and sometimes even into the opposite jaw. You can read more about this in the chapter 'Your rabbit's health'.

Differences

Although both belong to the hare-family, the hare and the rabbit are fundamentally different animals, not only in appearance, but also in reproduction and behaviour. The European hare is much bigger and heavier than the European rabbit, and it also has longer ears. The hare is a long distance runner, which can jump very high, whereas the rabbit is a very flexible sprinter. Hares make a nest on the ground (lair), and they are also found in the mountains. Rabbits, on the other hand, dig burrows and prefer flat land. Hares live solitary lives and look for a partner only when they want to reproduce. Rabbits live in big groups. Hares mate in full run, whereas

rabbits mate in a sitting position. Hares give birth to two to four young after approximately 43 days, and the young can run and see straight away (precocial). Rabbits give birth to more young (up to twelve) after approximately 30 days. Their young are naked, deaf and blind when born (nestling).

The European wild rabbit

As mentioned above, all the (dwarf) rabbit breeds descend from the European wild rabbit. This rabbit has a brown-grey colouring, which can be very uneven. The belly is white. The tail is almost black on top, and white underneath. The body is 35 to 50 centimetres long, the tail four to eight centimetres and the ears 6.5 to 7.3 centimetres. The European wild rabbit is found in western and central Europe, from Spain to southern Sweden and from Ireland to Hungary. In Italy, it is only found in a few areas. Wild rabbits live in open landscape, such as fields, meadows, dunes, heather fields, and sometimes in not too dense woods. They are not found in mountain regions above nine hundred metres. They prefer sandy ground.

Domestication

The Romans were the first to keep rabbits. They were not yet common in Italy during the Roman Empire. After the conquest of Spain, the Romans discovered how palatable rabbit flesh is. They captured rabbits and took them home. There, they were released into the wild. Later, the Romans built special rabbit cages, the leporaria, in which they could keep their rabbits.

In the Middle Ages, the rabbit was the favourite prey of the hunting elite. The animals were released onto small islands for that purpose. The Dutch zoologist Hans Nachtsheim did a lot of research into the domestication of the rabbit. He concluded that the first tame rabbits were bred in French monasteries. He based this on writings from the sixteenth century, in which different colourings are mentioned for the first time.

Domestication ensured that the tame rabbit soon differed from its wild cousins. The ears and eyes of the tame rabbit are not as efficient as those of the wild varieties, and it has 22 percent less brain. Tame rabbits can reproduce the whole year round, while their wild cousins can only give birth in spring.

Wild rabbits

Behaviour

Rabbits are animals with a characteristic behaviour. It is useful to know something about this.

Rabbits are gregarious animals in the wild. They can only survive in a group. A lot of the behaviour of the domesticated animal can be ascribed to the life in the wild. The so-called 'escape behaviour' is very characteristic for rabbits. Just as their wild cousins, domestic rabbits are most active at night. When worried, they "thump" on the ground with their hind legs as an alarm signal. In the wild, rabbits raise the alarm in the same way when danger is nearby.

As a rabbit is usually active in the evening, it is very quiet during the day. It is not good for the animal to try to change this behaviour too much. It disturbs its natural rhythm.

A rabbit is a clean animal, even in the wild. You can find 'natural lavatories', where the animals do their business every time. In captivity, a rabbit will always use the same corner of its cage.

Character

Most people think of the rabbit as a kind, gentle animal. Children, especially, love to cuddle their rabbits, but even adults can succumb to their charm. However, there can be big differences in behaviour, depending on the type of rabbit. An French Lop Rabbit is gentle and quiet, and therefore suitable for children. A Polish Rabbit, on the other hand, can be quite wild. Most pet shops sell the gentle varieties.

Company or cuddly toy

Some people buy a rabbit or another pet for their (small) children to play with. Live animals are, however, not toys. If you are looking for a cuddly toy for your children, buy one from a toyshop. However cute and soft a rabbit may be, you have to view it as a companion. It will not be happy if it is constantly patted, brushed and played with by children's hands. It will allow itself to be cuddled, but make sure that you find the middle ground by giving it the opportunity to run freely, with a night shelter in the form of an outdoor run. The children can then enjoy watching their favourite pet, without constantly pestering it.

Children and rabbits

The above is not intended to prevent you from buying a rabbit for a child. Rabbits are generally very good as 'children's animals'. When a young rabbit comes into the home, both children and rabbit have to get used to the new situation. The rabbit has to get used to being picked up by humans, while the children have to learn how to handle such a small animal. Let the children quietly hold their hand in the cage. The rabbit will sniff at it and maybe nibble at their fingers. Make sure that the child does not jump and pull its hand back quickly when the rabbit nibbles at a finger or a fingernail. The animal might really bite when frightened. Teach children, when

old enough, how to pick up a rabbit. Because of their excitement about their new companion, children are often boisterous and hectic, while the rabbit is also agitated. It is therefore important to limit the attention for the new housemate, as the rabbit will need its rest.

Picking up a rabbit

It is important to be calm when handling a rabbit. Never lift the animal by its ears. A rabbit can be picked up in two ways. When it is used to its environment and the people around it are calm, you can pick it up by lifting it from the ground with one hand between its back legs and the other hand under it's middle. Make sure that the rabbit cannot jump onto the ground. A rabbit can develop enough thrust with its hind legs to bruise or break its own vertebrae. The muscles in the hind legs are very powerful. If the rabbit is not calm enough, and does not want to be lifted, you can pick it up by holding it by the loose skin on its back (not just the neck) with one hand. This skin is called the 'scruff'. Put the rabbit's head on the other arm, and slide that hand under its back legs so that the animal can sit quietly.

Buying a rabbit

Pets, especially for children, are often bought on the spur of the moment. Mummy, look how cute! Which mother's heart would not be moved by the sight of cute rabbits and cute children?

The animal is then often bought without further thought about the consequences, and without enough information.

Obviously, this is not the ideal way to purchase a pet. It sometimes works out well, but more often it does not. Pets need a cage, food, medical care and anything else that adds up to care and attention, even when you come home after a tiring day at work, your children have to do homework, or a holiday is coming up. A child is often enthusiastic at the prospect of having an animal to care for. Once the novelty has faded however, the parents often have to take over.

On the other hand, a pet in the house can be very rewarding. It brings life into the home, and a piece of nature. A rabbit is also usually a kind, affectionate pet, which captures the hearts of adults and children alike. It is important that humans and animal suit each other. This is why you have to gather plenty of information about keeping your favourite pet. What sort of cage does it need, what sort of temperature, which food, what care, how much is it going to cost, have you got enough time? By answering all these questions before a possible purchase, you can prevent disappointments later. Never buy a pet if you are in any doubt.

One or more
If you want to buy a rabbit, one question then comes up: how many? Rabbits can easily be kept on their own. In this case, a fema-

le is an advantage. A buck can spread urine. This is also called 'spraying'. Males do this especially when they smell a female or have just mated one. If you want to keep several rabbits, think about it carefully. A male and female together will quickly have young. One nest of baby rabbits is cute. By the second or third time, all your neighbours, friends and family have already been supplied, and you cannot keep all the little ones yourself.

Just as male cats and dogs, a male rabbit can be castrated. This is, of course, expensive, and not every vet is willing to do such a fiddly job.

If you do choose to buy a couple, make sure that they are not related. If members of the same family reproduce, it is called inbreeding. This can cause damage to the young rabbits' health.
If you want two rabbits, but no young, choose two females. They are usually friendly to each other. If two males have been together since birth, it usually does not cause any trouble. It is, however, common enough that adult males attack each other.

If you want to breed rabbits, it is a good idea to become a member of a small animal breeders club. There will be experienced breeders there, who are willing to help beginners with tips and advice.

Things to watch out for

When you go to buy a rabbit, look out for the following:

- The animal must be healthy. A healthy rabbit has clean, bright eyes, clean genitals, clean ears, no unnatural lumps, a clean and dry nose, and clean lips without scabs.
- The fur should be smooth and shiny. There should be no wounds or flakes of skin.
- The rabbit has to be well fed, but not fat. It should feel solid, but should not have a high back or hollow flanks.
- Pay attention to the breathing. Piping or rattling breathing can be a sign of an infection. The nostrils should move calmly and

regularly during breathing.
• Droppings should be hard and dry. Wet, soft droppings can be a sign of an (intestinal) infection.
• The rabbit should not be too young. During the suckling period, the young get substances from their mother that give them immunity they badly need. Always ask their age and never buy an animal younger than eight weeks. Also, never buy an animal that seems too light for its age. On the other hand, an animal should also not be too old. Older animals, of course,

die sooner, but they also have more problems getting used to new surroundings. You can recognise older rabbits by their coat. It is often less glossy and sometimes displays bare patches.
• Also look at the other animals in the cage. If they look less lively or even sick, then the rabbit of your choice may also be harbouring an illness. Rabbits are vulnerable to infectious diseases. Try also to check that your animal is really the same sex as the salesperson told you. You can recognise full-grown males by

their small testicles. A breeder can carefully press out a young male's penis.

Where to buy

There are several places to buy a rabbit. Most are sold in a pet shop. Generally, the rabbits sold there are of good quality. You need to be aware, however, that there are good and not-so-good pet shops. Therefore, take a good look around the shop. Are the cages clean? Are the animals on offer healthy and active? Have they got plenty of clean drinking water? Do you get sufficient and, especially, honest information about the animals?

There are many rabbit breeders in this country. These try to breed 'perfect' examples for shows. If the rabbit does not meet the strict competition rules, they are selected at a young age to be sold. These animals are usually perfectly healthy, but may not be quite the right colour or build. Here too, it is important to be careful. There are some less good breeders around, who want their share of success. Your local small-animal club will be able to give you addresses of trustworthy breeders.

Sadly, there is another type of breeder. These people try to breed as many animals as they can as fast as they can, in an attempt to get rich quickly. Their 'victims' often live in draughty shelters,

with little room. Inbreeding and disease are common. These breeders often offer their animals for sale via advertisements and on markets. By buying from such people, you only help to keep such breeding factories running.

You can also buy a rabbit at one of the many breed shows, which are held primarily in the autumn and winter. These shows are worth visiting, even if you are not planning to buy a rabbit there.

Transport

If you are going to buy a rabbit, and you are well-prepared, you will probably take a transport box, a cage or a carton with you. Make sure that the animal is protected against draughts, rain and wind. Also make sure that there is plenty of ventilation. It is stressful enough for the young rabbit: separation from the mother, the stay in the shop, and then going on another journey with an unknown destination. Leave it in peace as much as possible during the first few days and give it the opportunity to get used to its new environment very slowly.

If you are picking your rabbit up with a car, do not let the animal stay in the hot sun while you go to do a quick errand. Even if the temperature outside does not seem high, it can get very warm in the car.

A home for your rabbit

Before we talk about your rabbit's new residence, it is interesting to know how rabbits live in the wild.

In the wild

Wild rabbits prefer to live in open areas and on sandy ground. They are very sociable animals, which live in big families. A rabbit family lives in a warren, and the bigger the family gets, the bigger the warren has to be.

The warren consists of the living room (the kettle), from which a number of passages spread out. These passages are divided into main passages and escape passages. One of the animals often looks for a higher point, from where it can spot danger.

Warrens are completely empty on the inside. The nesting chambers are quite a distance away from the living chamber. They are filled with dry grass, straw and fur, which the female plucks from her belly. After the birth, the mother visits the nesting chamber a few times a day to look after her young. After about thirty days the young leave the nesting chamber and integrate into the family.

Housing in captivity

You can keep your animals outdoors, but this is not advisable. You do not have as much contact with animals kept outdoors. The cage outside also has to be made resistant to the violent weathers of our climate. Animals kept outdoors also seem not to live as long as animals kept indoors.

A shed is a good alternative. It is certainly the best for the animal. Your rabbit grows a nice thick winter coat in a draught-free shed.

The air is also not too dry. Hobby breeders therefore always keep their animals in a shed or a stable. The lay rabbit owner has the disadvantage that a shed is still too far away from the living room. When it is raining, not everybody is happy to go outdoors. In this case, you also have too little contact with your rabbit, and it will feel lonely if it does not have others of its kind with it. A rabbit is a sociable animal that does not like to be alone.

A place in the house might be the best solution. The kitchen, especially a small one, is not the right place, as animals cannot cope with cooking smells, especially the smoke of oil or butter. Many people also find it unhygienic to keep an animal in the kitchen. The hallway is also inadvisable, as it is too draughty. A bedroom that is also used for other things during the day is a good choice. If the room is only used at night, the rabbit will feel lonely.

The best place is the living room, however. As mentioned above, rabbits are very sociable animals. They like to be in our company. You have to pay attention to a few things though:
A rabbit does not like noise. Whether it is rock, classical, or other music, it is still noise to the sensitive ears of your rabbit. People who enjoy loud music should find another spot for their

Protected from wind and rain

rabbit or wear headphones. Like most pets, rabbits do not like cigarette smoke. If people smoke in the living room, it is not the best place for your rabbit. The cage should not be in direct sunlight. The temperature can get extremely high, even in winter. Windows function like magnifying glasses.

Draughts are lethal for rabbits. It is therefore best not to put the cage on the ground. A place on a box or a table is preferable. Put the cage against a wall or in a corner to guarantee as much peace and quiet as possible for your ani-

mal. The animal feels safe if 'its back is covered'.

It should be obvious that a place next to an open fire or the central heating is also inadvisable.

Cage types

Anyone with a bit of patience and DIY talent can build a cage himself. It is of course easier to buy one in the pet shop. It does not make a big difference in price; the material for a DIY cage costs about the same as a ready-made example. The advantage of building a cage yourself is that you can adapt it completely to your

own wishes and ideas. Have you got a corner of 90 by 45 centimetres between two cupboards? You will have to search a long time for a cage to fit it. It can also be tricky to find the colour that will go perfectly with your interior.

Ready made cages in different sizes and styles are sold in pet shops and department stores. It is not always easy to decide. There are a few demands, which a cage should fulfil, even if you build it yourself:
• It should be a pleasant environment for the animal
• It must be big enough
• It must keep the animal contained
• There must be good air circulation
• Any mess must stay inside the cage
• It must be easy to clean
• It must be safe for animals and humans
• It must be easily accessible

A cage must be big enough to be a pleasant home for your animal. How big is big enough? Any cage is, really, a limitation to an animal's freedom, and is therefore never big enough. We must therefore find a good compromise between the

wishes of animal and human. The cage should not be too big for the human, but also not too small for the animal.

If your rabbit can run around outside its cage regularly, the following rule of thumb applies: A grown animal must be able to lie alongside the short side of the cage when it stretches out. The longer side of the cage is usually twice as long. You can find the minimum sizes in the table below: Obviously, a cage has to be strong enough to prevent escapes. The bars should therefore not be too far apart. Good ventilation is ensured by gauze or bars at the sides of the cage. Solid glass tanks are therefore inadvisable. The ammoniac fumes from the urine are caught on the ground.

The sides of the bottom tray must be at least fifteen centimetres high, to prevent too many droppings and shavings from falling out. However, you cannot completely prevent this from happening with rabbits.

To clean the cage thoroughly, you should be able to take it apart

Size of the cage

Type of rabbit	Weight (approximate)	Breadth	Depth	Height
Large breeds	> 4.5 kilos	100 cm	70 cm	60 cm
Medium breeds	2.5-5 kilos	70 cm	60 cm	60 cm
Small breeds	1.5-3 kilos	50 cm	50 cm	50 cm
Dwarf breeds	up to ca. 1 kilo	40 cm	50 cm	50 cm

easily. There should also be no sharp protrusions on either the outside or inside. You also need to be able to take out the feed bowl without too much trouble.

If you follow all the advice above, you will probably choose a cage which consists of a plastic tray with a wire top. This top section should have a large door at the front, and a 'lid' that you can remove.

Do-it-yourself

If you do decide to build a cage yourself, you can use several techniques and materials. As an example, we will describe the construction of a simple rabbit hutch. The hutch is made of plastic-covered chip board, approximately fifteen millimetres thick. You can buy this in any DIY store. You attach the side walls (48.5 x 45 centimetres) and the back wall (90 x 45 centimetres) to the floorboard (90 x 50 centimetres) with long, thin screws. At the bottom of the front wall, you attach a panel (87 x 15 centimetres) and a beam on the top (87 x 2 x 3 centimetres). Finally, you seal all seams with silicone, to prevent dampness getting into the component parts. The frame of the cage is now ready.

For the front, you need a frame, which you covered with gauze (87 x 27.5 centimetres). You close this front with three plugs in three holes at the bottom. You drill these holes into the top of the panel. At the top, the frame is kept in place by two pieces of wood, which you screw to the beam. Two pieces at the sides of the frame, behind the front, prevent the frame from falling in. For the top, too, you make a frame, which you can take out (87 x 45 centimetres), which you cover with mesh. This is the lid of the cage. To prevent this lid from falling in, you attach six small metal plates at the sides. You can hang a water bottle at the front of the cage.

Cage litter

Wood shavings have been used in animal cages for many years. This is often called sawdust but is actually shavings. Sawdust absorbs moisture exceptionally well and hardly smells, but a major disadvantage of sawdust is that it usually contains a lot of dust. Investigations in recent years have shown that this dust can seriously bother rodents. There are now many other types of cage litter on the market that are "healthier" for animals.

Sawdust

As we have said, sawdust is not very suitable as cage litter. Rabbits seem to have less problems with the dust than some other animals. This is probably because wild rabbits that always live on sandy ground can more easily close their respiratory organs to keep out fine sand and dust.

Now that the dust problem is generally recognised, some types of sawdust are cleaned better by the manufacturer. While sawdust is thus not unsuitable by definition, a better material is preferable, even if this is often more expensive. But never use sawdust from carpentry waste. This is often too fine in structure and may contain poisonous substances.

Hay

Rabbits like to use hay as nesting material and to chew on. It is an important part of their diet. Hay, however, does not absorb moisture well and is thus not really suitable as cage litter.

Luxury bedding

Straw

Straw is much too coarse to be suitable as cage litter or nest material for rabbits. There is a product on the market, which is made of shredded straw. Russell Rabbit is wonderfully soft and ideal as nesting material. However, it absorbs little moisture and is less suitable as cage litter.

Cat litter

There are probably a hundred different sorts of cat litter on the market. Some are suitable to keep rabbits or other rodents on, especially those made from maize. These absorb plenty of moisture and can do good service. Cat litter made of stone or clay is less suitable, mainly because it can become dusty.

Pressed pellets

In recent years various cage litters have appeared on the market that consist of pressed pellets. Some types have sharp edges and don't seem very comfortable.

Sand
Sand absorbs too little moisture to be used as cage litter. Apart from that, it gets dirty.

Shredded paper
There are also various types of shredded paper on offer as cage litter. These shreds are ideal to play with and can be used as nest material. But they absorb much too little moisture to be used as cage litter.
Never make cage litter yourself from old newspapers. The printing ink can poison your rabbit.

In conclusion, use a cage litter that easily absorbs moisture, in combination with a soft, insulating nesting material.

The interior
A rabbit cage must also contain a manger for its hay, which you can also buy ready-made at a pet shop. Water should be given in a drinking bottle that you hang on the outside, with the spout pointing into the cage. There are two small steel balls in the spout and by moving these the rabbit gets water. The spout should be of stainless steel, because rabbits sometimes gnaw on it. Any rabbit will quickly get used to a drinking bottle.

Use a heavy, stone dish for dry food. Rabbits like to stand at the dish with their forepaws on the edge. A dish that is too light will then easily tip over. Also useful to prevent tipping is a dish that is wider at the bottom than at the top. Green food can simply be laid in the cage.

It's a good idea to lay a piece of stone (paving slab) in the rabbit's regular running area. As the rabbit walks over it, it wears down its nails naturally.

Rabbits are clean animals that will pick their own toilet corner. Clean this corner every couple of days, then you will only need to clean the whole cage out every two weeks or so. Use an empty can to scrape clean the toilet corner.

Running free
A pet that is reasonably tame and kept in a smallish cage needs to be let out regularly for a run. Sufficient exercise is very important for an animal's health. If you let your rabbit run in the house, garden or balcony, you need to be aware of some dangers.

Watch out for electrical cables that an animal may gnaw on, poisonous houseplants, doors that may suddenly slam shut as well as dogs. Always keep a good eye on an animal running free.

Feeding your rabbit

The European wild rabbit enjoys a comprehensive menu. What's on offer depends on its habitat and the season. The whole year round, it likes to eat grasses, young twigs, leaves, and other pieces of plants.

Depending on the season, the menu may include fruits, berries, fungi, and buds. Very exceptionally, the wild rabbit eats animals, such as beetles. The changes of seasons ensure the necessary variety in its menu, and also ensure that changes in the diet do not happen too quickly. For our domesticated rabbits, a comprehensive menu is also important. A good diet consists of a certain amount of basic ingredients: hay, dry food, fresh food and water. You might add some special treats.

Hay

Hay is an important element in a healthy rabbit diet. Although it contains little in terms of nutrients, it's indispensable for the digestion. A rabbit must have fresh hay available every day. Apart from the so

important fibre (non-digestible elements in the food), it also contains calcium and magnesium. You can buy a bale of hay from a farmer or seed merchant, or in smaller packages from a pet shop.

Good, fresh hay contains young grass, clover and herbs. It is dry, but still a little green and smells wonderful. Poor quality hay contains practically no herbs, because it's often harvested from barren meadows. You can recognise old hay by its yellowish colour. It also gives off dust, which can be especially harmful to your animal's bronchial tracts. Apart from that, old hay contains no nutrients.

Dry foods

Dry food is a collective name for any food that is not fresh: loose grain types, mixed grain with grass kernels and ready-made pellets. You can buy maize, grain, barley, yeast, millet and various seeds at seed merchants. However, it's not worth the bother mixing your rabbit's food yourself. Ready-made rabbit grain mixtures contain everything your animal needs for a balanced diet. These mixed foods also contain grass pellets. Experience shows that rabbits eat these pellets last, so it's important that they get precisely the amount of food that they eat in one day. If anything is left over, give them somewhat less the next day.

There are also ready-made pellets in the shops. These pellets are all identical in their composition. They contain all the necessary nutrients and provide a perfect diet, without having to find and wash green vegetables. But apart from the ease of use, it must be pretty boring for a rabbit to have to eat the same food every day.

Seed and grains have a high nutritional value. A rabbit that gets too much mixed grain and too little green food and exercise can quickly get fat. In that case you can happily let your pet 'fast' one or two days a week. Only give it

Hay with herbs

Cabbage may cause problems

hay and water on these days. Whatever food you choose, always watch for the date of manufacture. Food that is older than three months loses a large portion of its nutritional value.

Green foods

Rabbits in the wild eat more green foods than grain, so green foods must make up a substantial part of the diet for a pet rabbit. Here we mean those green foods that are suitable for a rabbit. This list is almost inexhaustible, but never take a risk if in any doubt. Only give your rabbit things that you're sure it can eat.

You can find wild herbs in woods and meadows. Don't pick green foods for your pet alongside roads or in areas with heavy industry, as these plants are probably contaminated with lead and other poisons. Also avoid agricultural land, because of insecticides. To avoid any risk, wash any green food thoroughly, then let it drain and dry a little.

You can give your rabbit practically any fruit or vegetable, although some cabbage varieties can cause intestinal problems. Greenhouse lettuce contains a lot of nitrate, so give cabbage and lettuce only in small quantities.

Carrots are the most commonly known rabbit food, but too many can cause diarrhoea. Do not feed a rabbit more than one carrot per day. It is the rule for most fresh food that too much can cause problems.

Water

That rabbits need only a little to drink is a fable. Even if you give them plenty of green food, they still need fresh water every day. Give them water at room temperature in a drinking bottle. Clean the bottle regularly as poisonous algae

Poisonous	Less suitable	Suitable fresh food	Fruit	Vegetables
Laburnum	White cabbage	Field plants	Carrots	Apples
Poison hemlock	Red cabbage	Dandelion leaves	Carrot leaves	Pears
Yew	Cauliflower	Clover	Lamb's Lettuce	Bananas
Deadly Nightshade	Red Clover	Plantain	Endives	Kiwis
Potato seeds	Cabbage Lettuce	Thistle	Chicory	Raspberries
Kidney beans	Raw potato	Plucked gras	Giant white radish leaves	Strawberries
	Mown grass	Young stinging nettles	Celery	Grapes
		Jerusalem Artichoke	Turnip cabbage	Cherries
			Fennel	Plums
			Sunflower	Parsley
			Spinach	
			Sweet Corn	

can build up inside it. Rabbits sometimes have the habit of drinking from their bottle with a mouth full of food, so it can become dirty or blocked. Check the bottle and replace the water every day.

Ten golden rules for good feeding

1. A rabbit cannot decide itself how much and what it has to eat. It can hardly or never detect poisonous food, and can become very fat very quickly.
2. A varied menu is very important. This ensures that your rabbit gets plenty of nutrients.
3. Just as humans do, rabbits also like to eat regularly. They prefer to eat twice a day (dry food in the morning and fresh food in the afternoon).
4. Wash all fresh food and let the water drain off.
5. Remove any fresh food and fruit, which has not been eaten within half an hour. It will go mouldy and litter the cage.
6. Never collect fresh food at the sides of roads.
7. Beware of possible agricultural chemicals.
8. Never feed frozen or cooked food.
9. Do not change your rabbit's menu too quickly.
10. A good diet consists of hay, mixed grains, fresh food, water and something to gnaw on. This will ensure that your rabbit stays healthy.

Snacks and treats

Although the rabbit is not a rodent, it does have incisors. To keep its teeth in good condition it needs something to gnaw on. There are various munchies available in pet shops, but you can also use branches or twigs from willow, fruit or other deciduous trees. A hard slice of dried bread or some crispbread are also suitable snacks.

Waterbottle

Don't give a rabbit crisps, biscuits, sweets or sugar lumps as extras. These are extremely unhealthy for pets, as they contain too much salt, sugar and fat. There are enough healthy snacks that you can use to give your rabbit a treat. Of course, not every animal has the same tastes, one rabbit may like something that another won't eat, but parsley, chicory, carrot leaves, rose-hips and kiwis will usually bring a smile to their faces. With a well-balanced diet, you don't need to add any extra vitamins or minerals. But it is a good idea to give rabbits a so-called salt stone or licking block. They will use them automatically if they're lacking salt or minerals

Pet shops carry a large assortment of snacks

Salt stone

Shows

Many people breed rabbits as a hobby. They take them to small-animal shows, where they hope to win prizes with their finest examples, but the rabbit's appearance, colour and coat are subject to strict rules; not everything is permitted. The perfect rabbit fulfils the standards of the breeders' association.

The Standard

The breeders' association standard describes how rabbits and other small rodents such as the Guinea Pig, the Golden Hamster, the Mongolian Gerbil and the tame rat or fancy mouse should ideally look.

An animal entered for a competition can earn points in seven categories. In the table you can see how many points a rabbit can score in each category. Points are deducted for any defects depending on their seriousness. The animal that finally scores the most points is the winner and earns the title 'best in show'.

Rabbits come in many more colourings and markings than those included in the standard.

But a colouring or marking is only officially recognised if it's in the standard.

It is also possible to enter the animal as a 'new colour' for the standard. There are a number of requirements that a colour or marking must meet to be included. At least four animals with the new colour or marking must be entered for

Points awarded for the rabbit		
Type and build	20	points
Weight	10	points
Coat and condition	20	points
Head	15	points
Ears	15	points
Colour	15	points
Physical condition	5	points
	100	points

the federation's show. There they are judged and possibly approved by the standards committee of the association. The first step is preliminary recognition. If, after three years, there are enough animals with the new colour or marking, it is then fully recognised.

Judging

During judging, the animals entered are judged on the following points:

Type and build

This part of the standard describes a rabbit's build. This is again different for each breed. You can read more about the various breeds, colourings and markings in the chapter "Breeds and Colourings".

Weight

When judging, an animal's weight, its age and, of course, the breed is taken into account.

Coat and hair condition

This part of the standard varies per variety and hair structure. A show animal must have a full coat, laid flat and glossy, that means no thin or bald patches. Any moulting costs points and can be recognised by lack of guard hairs. These are the harder support hairs that are shed first.

All scores are noted

Judging the animals

The new coat, which is longer and more intense in colour, is clearly visible. A few loose hairs are not a problem, but loose lumps are marked as moulting.

Head and ears

This section is also judged per variety and markings. You can find more details in the following chapter.

Topcoat and belly colour

The topcoat is understood to be the surface colour on the animal's back. The word 'surface' is very important here. A hair usually consists of different colours. The base of a hair (at the body) will have a certain colour. In certain cases the intermediate part of the hair will have its own colour. The top and belly colours are important because the colour of the hair tip is obviously the most visible. The various top and belly colours are described in the colouring descriptions.

Middle and base colour

After reading the above, it should be clear what is meant by interme-

The weighing
of the rabbit

diate and base colour. These colours can be seen by blowing into the coat. The hairs lay back, forming a kind of rosette that clearly shows the base, intermediate and topcoat colours.

Body condition and care
In this section the general impression that the rabbit makes will be judged. A rabbit should feel muscular and powerful. Sloppy, thin or fat animals will be judged poorly. Nails must be clipped, the coat clean and free of tangles. The eyes must be clean and bright. Sick or injured animals are marked down as extremely serious faults. The same applies to visibly pregnant animals.

Rabbit breeds

There are many rabbit types. Just as with dogs, they are classified into different breeds. The breeds are split into large, medium and small breeds. There is a separate group for breeds with special hair structure.

Flemish Giant

Giant breeds
These include the very large and heavy rabbits.

British Giant
The British Giant is the biggest rabbit breed in the world. It is approximately 80 cm long and weighs around seven kilos. They are not advisable as pets for children, as children find it difficult to look after such a heavy animal. They are closely related to the Flemish Giant rabbit in Europe. British Giants are bred in white, steel-grey, agouti, opal and fawn.

Giant Papillon
The Giant Papillon is very quiet. A smaller spotted variety, the English, is more advisable for children. The ears of the Great English are at least 16 centimetres long, and should stand up straight. The Great English has a particular marking on its white coat. It has a 'butterfly' on its nose, rings around the eyes, a 'thorn' exactly in the middle of the nose bone, patches on the cheeks, and completely coloured eyes. It has a dorsal stripe, which runs from behind the ears to the tail. On both sides, the rabbit has patches that are round, and do not touch each other. The Giant Papillon can be black, blue, chocolate and lilac.

French Lop
French Lops are quiet, kind animals, with a very balanced temperament. It is sometimes found as a children's pet. French Lops have a firm, compact and muscular body with a wide chest. The ears are thick and fleshy and small knots,

the so-called crowns, are found at the base of the ears. The French Lop is found in various colours, including agouti, chinchilla, black, blue and broken-coloured.

Large to Medium breeds
This group is the largest group of pedigree rabbits.

Chinchilla Giganta
The Chinchilla Giganta is a quiet rabbit that gives birth to large litters. It is popular with hobby breeders who want to improve the breed. Chinchilla Gigantas have a white base colour with black ticking, while the belly is always white. A standardisation of the Chinchilla has not yet been successful at international level.

New Zealand
Contrary to what the name implies, the New Zealand has its origins in the US. They are quiet, reliable rabbits, and the females are good mothers, which can give birth to many young. New Zealands can have white or black coats.

English Lop
The English Lop is more popular in some countries than in others. It is not usually kept as a pet, and not everybody likes this particular type of rabbit. The long ears also need special care. English Lops are usually found in the Sooty Fawn colouring, but also in agouti and steel-grey.

Burgundy Yellow
This big and heavy breed is not usually kept as a pet in the UK. A small group of hobby breeders are still attempting to improve the breed, especially in the Netherlands, where the coat is yellow, whereas it is usually a little redder in other countries.

Argente Champagne
The Argente Champagne is a very quiet rabbit, and the tips of its hair makes it look silver. The coat is longer than usual and has a lot of underwool, which makes this rabbit feel very soft. It can be black, blue, brown or yellow in colour.

Belgian Hare, Belgian Hare Black and Tan and Belgian Hare White
The Belgian Hare has nothing in common with the wild hare. However, its elegant appearance does have similarities with the hare, which is how it got this name. It did not in fact originate in Belgium, but in England. Belgian Hares are lively and affectionate and are good pets and breeding animals.

Californian
Californians are very friendly and reliable rabbits, but too big to be popular pets. The colouring of this breed stands out. They have a white body with coloured extremities (paws, nose, ears and tail). They can be black, blue or lilac.

Giant Papillon

English Lop

Argente Champagne

New Zealand white

Belgian Hare

Meissner Lop

Meissner Lops are quiet and affectionate rabbits, which are not very well known to the public. They are most common in Germany. The Meissner Lop can be agouti, black, yellow, blue and brown. Breeders try to achieve a silvery sheen, which should be as even as possible. This silvering develops at around five to six weeks of age.

Vienna (coloured) and Vienna (white)

Coloured and white Viennas are extremely popular on the Continent where they are found at basically all exhibitions. They are also very popular as (children's) pets. They are becoming more popular in the UK. The coloured Vienna can be blue to hare coloured and from black to rabbit grey. White Viennas have a shiny white coat and light blue eyes.

Beveren (blue) and Beveren (white)

Beverens are very lively rabbits. The rear paw is visibly higher than the front, and it is also more muscular. Hobby breeders, especially, like this breed. The blue colour is strikingly blue, and the Beveren has a lot of underwool, which makes it feel very soft.

Blanc de Hotot

The 'Hotot' is one of the most difficult rabbits to breed to perfection. The black eye-rings, which should be perfectly circular, are very difficult to achieve. Although they have a friendly nature, they are not popular as pets. There are coloured dwarfs with the same markings in Europe, which are far more popular.

New Zealand Red

New Zealand Reds are quiet, although they are more active than the white and black New Zealands. They are particularly popular as show animals. New Zealand Reds have a deep red colour and no markings or white hair.

Silver Fox

The Silver Fox is particularly popular because of its rich, soft and elastic fur. It is common as a show animal worldwide, but not very popular as a pet. The Silver Fox is found in black, brown and blue.

Harlequin

The Harlequin is a French breed and it is generally very friendly. They are not common as children's pets as they are very big and heavy. They have striking two-coloured striped markings, which makes them difficult to breed. One colour is always yellow to yellow-red, the other can be black, brown, blue or lilac.

Magpie

The Magpie is actually a Harlequin with white instead of yellow-red patches. It is very big and difficult to breed. Luck plays

Californian

Beveren blue

Blanc de Hotot

New Zealand red

Harlequin

Rhinelander

Thuringer

Sallander

English

a major role in the breeding of this variety. It is not very popular as a pet, probably because of its size and because it is not very well known.

Rhinelander

Rhinelanders are friendly rabbits, which are often kept as pets for adults and children alike. They have black and yellow-red markings with dark brown eyes, or blue and yellow markings with blue eyes. The special markings on the white coat are typical for this breed.

Thuringer

The Thuringer is a very friendly rabbit, which is particularly popular on the European mainland. It is popular with hobby breeders, and can be seen at many shows. It is not as common in England and the US. The rabbit is yellow-brown, and each hair has a dark tip. This gives its coat a subtle haze, which should not be too dark. The colour is darker on the ears, breast, nose, back legs, paws, belly, the lower part of the shoulders and the flanks than on the rest of the body. This colour is known in other breeds as Sooty Fawn.

Sallander

The Sallander is similar to the Thuringer, but with lighter colours. It is beige coloured with darker points and shadings. This colour is known as Seal Point in Dwarf Lops. They are not very popular as pets.

English

The English is one of the most striking and most popular breeds. It is very common as a pet because of its pretty appearance and its handy size. It is friendly, affectionate, and lively. English rabbits are found in various colours and have special head and body markings. They have spots on the flanks and butterfly marks on the nose, eye-rings and cheek spots on the head. The ears are fully coloured.

Havana

Havanas are usually kept by hobby breeders. They aim to standardise the type, the coat and the colour and to improve it. Havanas are not common pets, although they make very good companions. The Havana's colour should be a chocolate brown as dark as possible. The eyes have a red glow, the so-called fireglow, in a certain light.

Alaska

This rabbit has its name from the original breeding goal: to breed a black rabbit with white hair tips, just like the Alaska fox. Alaskas are lively animals and not very common as pets. The body is jet black, but slightly lighter on the belly and the breast. The eyes are dark brown.

Gouvenor

The Gouvenor is a quiet, affectionate animal. It is a very good pet, although not yet known in the UK. Gouvenors are a pastel-like light blue (lilac), and have a red glow to their eyes in a particular light.

Lux
The Lux is a real show rabbit on the European Continent. Rabbit lovers try to improve the type and colour. It also makes a very good pet. It has a special coat: the base colour is white, the intermediate colour is a warm yellow-red, and the tips of its hair are silver-blue.

Pearlfee
The Pearlfee is a friendly, good-natured, lively animal. The shiny coat feels soft and elastic. The coat of the Pearlfee is unique. This rabbit is blue grey with hair tips in different colours. The effect of these different colours is called 'pearling', which is how

this breed got its name.

Beige
The Beige is most common in the Netherlands and in England. It is usually kept by hobby breeders. Beiges are companionable and reliable rabbits. They have a yellow coat, and some of their hair has pastel blue tips.

Marburger Feh
The Marburger Feh is a lively and friendly rabbit. It is most common in Europe. The colour is blue with a subtle brown haze.

Deilenaar
The Deilenaar is a firm, strong rabbit. It is normally kept by hobby breeders, but it also makes a good pet. Its colour is a warm red-brown with an irregular black marking.

Gouvenor

Lux

Pearlfee

Marten Sables

Marten Sables are lively animals with a friendly character. They have creamy-white markings on their belly, noses and the inside of the ears. Their pleasing colour, friendly character and handy size make them popular pets. The Marten comes in various colours, including blue, sepia brown and yellow.

German Lop

The German Lop is a fairly new breed, roughly intermediate in size between a French Lop and a Dwarf Lop. They are quiet and good-natured animals and there-fore ideal pets. German Lops are bred in many different colours, including agouti, steel-grey and chinchilla.

Small breeds

Although dwarf breeds also exist, this book only names the small breeds.

Small Lotharinger

The Small Lotharinger is very popular in the Netherlands, but not seen in the UK. It is a lively and good-natured animal. Breeders breed different varieties in different countries, for example the Czech Lotharinger and the Kleinschecken (Germany).

Tan

The Tan is an extremely popular rabbit. The breed characteristics are the special reddish-brown markings on the belly, face, feet

and ears. It is very friendly and is often kept as a pet. The most com-mon top colour is black, followed by blue and brown and lilac.

Thrianta

The Thrianta is loved by a small enthusiastic group of breeders. As it is not very well known, it is not often found as a pet, although its friendly character and its handy size would make it a very good one. The Thrianta is as deep orange red as possible, with dark brown eyes.

Dutch

The Dutch is one of the oldest known rabbit breeds. It is very popular as a pet. This is due to its special markings (two-coloured head patches, which cover the eyes, the cheeks and the ears, and a coloured hindquarters), the variety of colours and its quiet and companionable character.

Silver

The Silver is probably one of the oldest rabbit breeds in the world. It is a lively animal, which makes it less suitable as a children's pet. It is very popular with exhibitors and is characterised by having lots of white hairs scattered through-out the coat. The base colour can be black or agouti.

Hulstlander

The Hulstlander is a new breed with Dutch origins and not yet well known in the UK. It has a white coat and blue eyes. It is

German Lop

Tan

Small Chinchilla

Rabbit breeds

Swiss Fox

Satin

Himalayan

Angora

Rex Dalmatian

very lively and therefore less suitable for children.

Himalayan

Like many breeds, the Himalayan hails from the UK. They are quiet and friendly. This little rabbit is very popular with breeders and also makes a very good pet. Himalayans are only marked on their extremities, which include ears, nose, paws and tail. They can be black, blue or Havana brown.

Breeds with a special coat structure

Some breeds are distinguished by their coat.

Rex

The Rex is not common as a pet. This is a shame as they are good-natured and have a very short, soft, velvety coat. The Rex is found in a large number of colours, both standard size and mini-rex.

Angora

The Angora is the oldest rabbit breed as far as we know. It has to be brushed carefully every day to prevent the coat from tangling. Its coat has to be clipped or cut regularly, usually once every three months. Angoras come in different colours. It is remarkable that the colour can only be seen well in the shorter coat of adult animals, around the nose and in the ears. The rest of the body is far paler in colour.

Angora rabbits have a long coat, which can be sheared, just as with sheep. Angora wool is very soft and doesn't itch as much as sheep wool. It is also warmer. If you want to keep angora rabbits, you should also learn how to shear them. If a coat has not been clipped for a while, it grows long and gets tangled. You can clip an Angora rabbit when the fur is at least ten centimetres long. This takes 10 to 13 weeks. An average Angora rabbit produces more than one kilogram of wool per year.

These rabbits need to be groomed regularly to keep their coat in good shape. Angora wool can be spun just like sheep's wool. The wool is ideal for making beautiful clothing.

Satin

The Satin is a quiet and good-natured animal. Since its origins, the Satin has been kept primarily by hobby breeders. It has a unique sheen to the coat. The Satin makes a very good children's pet, but is not yet well known. The Satin rabbit is bred in many colours, ivory being the most popular.

Swiss Fox

The Swiss Fox is a quiet animal and the ideal solution for people who want a rabbit with (medium) long hair, but do not want to spend a lot of time grooming it. Swiss Foxes are bred in different colours. White animals with blue or red eyes are the most popular.

Colourings

Rabbit grey

Small animal breeders experiment a lot with different colours. It is often not easy to describe a colour precisely, because there are many nuances. This is why many colours are described precisely in the standard. Rabbits have to fulfil this standard to win prizes.

Ticking
The mixed or spotty effect of many wild animals is called ticking. This pattern is normally most obvious on the back. The tips of the hairs are black or dark grey.

Hare coloured
Hare coloured animals have the colour of wild animals, but with a little more red. The back shows a nice regular ticking. Small-animal breeders distinguish between colours with and without ticking.

Rabbit grey
This colour looks like that of the wild rabbit with black ticking. The colour should not be too dark. The belly is white with a blue base colour. The eyes are dark brown.

Iron grey
The hair on the back is light grey with black ticking. The grey with the black should form a warm colour. The tail is almost black on top and the eyes are dark brown.

Brown grey
This colour is almost identical to rabbit grey, but the ticking should be brown instead of black. The belly is white and the eyes are brown.

Blue grey
As rabbit grey, but with blue ticking. The belly is white with a blue under-colour and the eyes are blue-grey.

Chocolate smoke
As iron grey, but with brown ticking. The eyes are brown.

Blue smoke
As iron grey, but with blue tic-king. The eyes are blue grey.

Black
The black has to be of a very intensive colour over the whole body. The belly may be a little lighter, and the eyes are dark brown.

Chocolate
In small animal breeding, brown is the colour of dark chocolate. The eyes are dark brown with a red glow, which can be difficult to see.

Blue
This colour is described as a shiny steel blue spread over the whole body. The eyes should be blue grey.

Yellow
This is a warm yellow colour, without any black hair. The belly is white and the ears are brown.

Orange
This is a warm orange-red colour spread over the whole body. The colour is a little lighter on the belly. The eyes are dark brown.

Chinchilla
This colour is named after the chinchilla, a Cavia variety with a superb coat. The mixed, black & light grey hair leads to an irregular ticking. This silver-grey colour covers almost the whole body. The eyes are dark brown. The chinchilla colouring results from the wild colouring and rabbit grey, without the influence of yellow.

Hare coloured

Black

Markings

Just as rabbits can have different colours, they can also have different markings. A rabbit may have inherent markings and/or individual markings. The following markings are distinguished in the standard:

Hotot

This is a white rabbit with black eye rings. The ring may be between three and five millimetres wide.

Japanese

The Japanese marking belongs to the breed of the same name. It is a mixed marking: one ear is dark or black, the other light. One side of the head is dark, the other light. The same applies to the paws. The back is striped red-black over the width.

Dutch

This pattern, too, is named after a breed. A rabbit with this pattern has two identical patches over the head, each including the ear and the cheek. The ears are dark. The front of the body is white, the back darker. The front paws are white and the darker hind paws have a white ring.

Himalayan

The Himalayan pattern is also named after a breed. The white rabbit has dark extremities (tail, paws, ears and tip of nose). This pattern is also common on guinea pigs and fancy mice.

To judge the colours well, judges blow a rosette into the coat

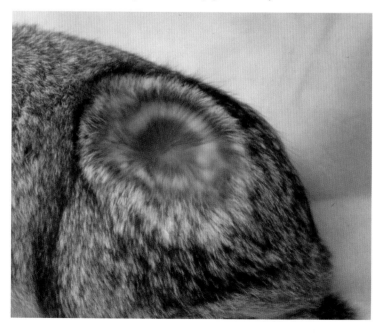

Silvering

For silvering, half of each hair is silver, which makes them appear to be jumping out. The silvering should be evenly spread.

Besides the variable markings, there are also markings that are more strictly described. The following types are described in the standard:

Madagascar

This consists of a yellow brown topcoat, with brown tips. This gives it a light red shine, which should not be too dark. The belly is almost black, just as over the nose, breast, paws, ears and the lower part of the shoulders, flanks and backhand. The basic colour of the belly is white to crème. The eyes and whiskers are dark brown.

Isabella

This pattern is lighter than Madagascar. The hair tips are blue. The rest is the same as Madagascar.

Silver fox

This pattern is named after the silver fox type of fur. A silver fox rabbit is dark with a white belly. The inside of the ears, an eye ring, a spot on the nose and a triangle in the neck are white.
The so-called 'spots' are a speciality of the silver fox. These are bright white hairs on the animal's flanks, which become more dense the closer they are to the white

Himalayan pattern

belly. These spots give the animal its attractive appearance.

Marten

This pattern is similar to that of the Russian. These rabbits have a light skin colour, but not white. The boundaries between colours are also not as clearly defined.

Tan

This pattern is named after the breed with the same name, which was formerly known as 'black-and-tan'. This is a jet black rabbit with a fiery rust-red breast, belly and eye ring.
The colour boundaries are clearly defined. Lighter coloured animals also have a lighter tan colour on the belly.

Reproductio

Whenever you keep a male and a female rabbit together, you are almost guaranteed offspring. You should think very carefully from the very beginning whether you really want to start breeding.

A litter of baby rabbits is very cute, but after the second and third time, it will be very difficult to find good homes for the babies. Therefore, be aware of all the aspects of reproduction when you buy your animals and decide whether you want to breed or not. If you have got a male and a female rabbit, but you do not want to breed, you can keep them in separate cages. It is also possible to have the male castrated.

Male or female

It is not easy to determine a rabbit's sex at a glance. Experienced rabbit owners know a trick: They hold the rabbit upside down on their lap, and push the skin folds at the genital opening aside. A male rabbit will have a small penis. If you cannot tell the sex

yourself, you can ask at a pet shop or vet's. It is quite common that a novice sales assistant makes a mistake in determining the sex, and the two 'females' all of a sudden have babies.

In-breeding

A responsible breeder will never mate any male with any female, because of the risk of in-breeding. For example, if you've got a brother and sister from neighbours, it's best not to mate them. If these animals produce young, this is a serious form of in-breeding and who can guarantee that the neighbour's litter wasn't also produced by a brother and sister?

One occasion of in-breeding is certainly not a disaster, but several times in succession will quickly

show the results. The young become smaller and weaker with each litter, fewer young are born and congenital abnormalities can also appear.

Mating
Spring is the best time to breed rabbits. Make sure that the doe is at least six months old before she is covered. A doe has to be in season before she can be covered. You can tell whether she is ready or not by her behaviour. She digs into the straw, builds nests and is generally very hectic. Do not let a strange ram into the doe's cage

straight away. Put the cages next to each other for a few days, so that the animals can smell and see each other. Then put them together in a 'neutral' cage or (preferably) a room. The ram will try to win the doe over with lots of begging and macho-behaviour. The animals sniff each other intensively and the male licks the female. He often runs around her grumbling, and lifting her tail. Finally, the female presses herself flat to the ground with her hindquarters raised. The actual mating process takes fifteen to twenty seconds. Try to plan for the birth, and

therefore note the date when mating has taken place.

Pregnancy and birth

After successful mating, it takes approximately ten hours before the fertilised egg nestles into the uterus. The rabbit's pregnancy lasts 31 to 32 days. The female will need plenty of rest in this period. She should no longer be picked up. She also needs extra feed and minerals. Give her a lick stone, which contains salts and minerals. The mother-to-be knows instinctively what she needs to eat, and she will get the supplements she needs by licking the stone. A few days before the birth, clean the cage thoroughly and offer plenty of nesting material.

The birth normally proceeds smoothly. The mother places the

young in the nest, which she has prepared in advance. Sometimes an inexperienced mother gives birth to her young in different parts of the cage, and leaves them to their fate. In this case, place the young in the nest with the help of a cloth or a textile glove. Never touch the young with bare hands or leather gloves, as the mother will reject the young because of the scent.

After the birth, the mother will eat the afterbirth. This behaviour is instinctive and is a left-over from life in the wild. By eating the placenta, she takes in extra nutrients. It also prevents predators from smelling the afterbirth and attacking the young. Usually three to four young are born, but it can be up to eight. It is advisable to check for dead babies in the nest. Do this very carefully, as a threatened doe can be very aggressive towards humans and animals approaching her young.

Development

After the first check, you should leave the nest alone for a few days. Check again after four days. In most cases, the young will be lying in their nest with full bellies. Sometimes there's one animal left behind, which is obviously smaller and thinner. This animal will normally survive, but will remain smaller and thinner. The first fur is visible after a few days. They open their eyes at around the tenth day. Keep this in mind, but do not try to open the eyes too early. The young should grow quickly. Their weight will have doubled after a week, and after two weeks their weight is four times their birth-weight. You can start to feed them after a month. Special food for young rabbits is available in pet shops.

Bottle-rearing

If the young remain thin and lean, the mother does not have enough milk. You can supplement it. If the mother dies after birth or rejects her young, you can try to rear them with a bottle yourself. This is only successful if they had their mother's milk after birth. You can buy small bottles designed for rearing kittens in the pet shop, which you can also use for rearing rabbits. You can even buy special rabbit rearing milk in powder form. Rabbits that have been raised with a bottle will be extremely affectionate, but the whole process is very time-consuming and laborious.

Depending on the mother's lactation, the babies have to be fed two to four times a day. After feeding, their bellies should be massaged with a damp Q-tip to encourage digestion. The mother does this by licking the bellies and genitals of her young.

Your rabbit's health

There are a few rules to adhere to if your rabbit is ill: If the animal lives together with others in the same cage, remove it as quickly as possible. It may be infectious with a risk for your other animals.

Keep your animal in a quiet, semi-dark place. Stress, crowding and noise will not help it get better. Keep it warm, but make sure its surroundings are not too hot. The best temperature is 18 to 21° C. Do not wait too long before visiting a vet. Rabbits that get sick have little will to survive and sometimes die within a few days.

The patient should always have fresh water, and remember that your animal may be too weak to reach its water bottle. Sick animals often eat little or nothing. Give it a small piece of apple or other fruit. Rabbits fortunately generally have few problems with their health. A healthy rabbit looks alert and is lively. Its coat is smooth, soft and regular. The anal area is dry and clean. A sick rab-

bit always sits withdrawn. The coat is dull and stands up as if it were wet. The animal has a raised back, even when moving.

The old saying 'prevention is better than a cure' is especially true with small animals, such as rabbits. It is not always easy to treat a sick rabbit. Even a slight cold can be fatal for your rabbit. The biggest dangers are therefore draughts and damp.

Colds and pneumonia
Draughts are the most common cause of colds and pneumonia for rabbits, so choose the place for its home carefully.

They can withstand low temperatures relatively well, but cold in combination with a draught almost inevitably leads to a cold. A rabbit starts sneezing and gets a wet nose. If its cold gets worse, the animal starts to breathe with a rattling sound and its nose will run even more, so it's now high time to visit the vet, who can prescribe antibiotics. A rabbit with a cold or pneumonia must be kept in a draught-free and warm room (18 to 21° C).

Diarrhoea

Diarrhoea is another formidable threat to rabbits and often ends fatally. Unfortunately, diarrhoea is usually the result of incorrect feeding, sometimes in combination with draughts or damp. Some cases of diarrhoea are caused by giving the animal food with too high moisture content. Rotted food or dirty drinking water can also be a cause. You can do a lot yourself to prevent diarrhoea.

Should your rabbit become a victim then you must take any moist food out of the cage immediately. Feed your animal only dry bread, boiled rice or crispbread. Replace its water with lukewarm camomile tea. Clean out its cage litter and nest material twice a day. As soon as the patient is completely recovered, you must disinfect its cage.

Coccidiosis

This common intestinal disorder is a threat especially to young animals. They are very vulnerable at the age of six to eight weeks.

Myxomatosis victim

Coccidiosis is an illness, which runs through several phases. It is caused by the so-called 'o-cyst'. This is a trace element which reproduces in the rabbit's intestines. Hygiene, ambient temperature and damp are major factors for the development of this illness. There are different types of coccidiosis. Symptoms include loss of weight and a bloated abdomen. Early medical intervention can save the animal's life.

Myxomatosis

Myxomatosis is one of the most common diseases amongst wild rabbits. It is spread via midges, fleas and ticks. At the beginning of an infection, the eyelids swell up. A gel-like fluid develops, which later turns into pus. The eyes stick together very quickly and finally the whole face swells up. An infected animal will die within ten days or so. This disease is basically not treatable. Preventive vaccination, however, is possible. If you keep your rabbits outdoors in an area where myxomatosis is prevalent, it is advisable to have your rabbit vaccinated.

VHD (Viral Haemorrhagic Disease)

This disease is highly contagious and has been brought into Europe from the Far East via the import of infected rabbit meat from China. Younger animals are not as vulnerable as older ones. There is,

however, no guarantee that they will not catch it. The symptoms are obstructed respiration, haemorrhaging with blood from the nose and paralysis. The animal dies a few days later. Medical treatment is not possible, but a vaccination is available from your vet. This offers protection in most cases, but not all. In a post-mortem, kidney and liver disorders can be detected.

Snot

Snot looks like a beginning cold, but can cause painful death within a few days. With this bacterial disease, hygiene and bad shelter (cold, draughty cages) play an important factor. Shortly after the first symptoms (sneezing and rattling), a watery excretion comes out of the nose. This excretion turns into pus, and the sneezing increases. At this point, a visit to the vet's is of utmost importance. If not treated, the rabbit will have trouble breathing and will die within a week. Snot develops very slowly, and affected animals lose a lot of weight.

Tumours

Rabbits are generally not particularly prone to tumours. If they do appear, it is usually at a higher age. Tumours are mostly found in families where a lot of inbreeding has occurred. The most common tumours affect the mammary glands of females. A tumour can also be the result of skin cancer.

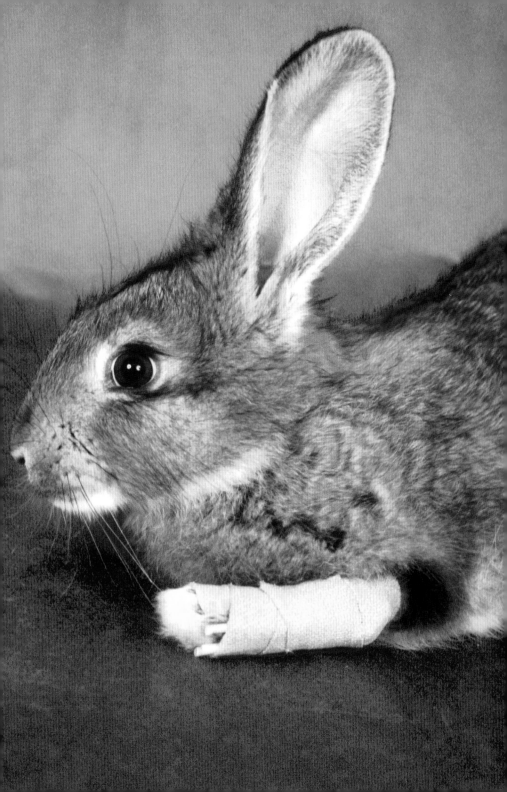

These forms can be removed surgically, but this might not be advisable because of the animal's advanced age. Another form of tumour is caused by an infection under the skin, which is called an abscess. A small wound may heal, but an infection remains under the skin. This type of tumour can easily be treated by a vet who opens and cleans it. Should your rabbit show signs of a tumour, take it straight to the vet's. Delaying can only make things worse, both with skin cancer and abscesses.

Broken bones

Rabbits sometimes break bones because they get stuck with their paws, jump off your hand or fall from a table. An animal with a broken paw will not put weight on it and will limp around the cage.

If it's a "straight" fracture (the paw is not deformed), this will heal within a few weeks. Take care that the rabbit can reach its food and drink without difficulty. If a rabbit has broken its back, it's best to have it put to sleep. If in doubt about a possible fracture, always ask your vet.

Long teeth

Teeth malformations

Rabbits that are fed a diet with too few minerals run the risk of broken teeth. If you notice that your rabbit has a broken tooth, check that its diet is properly balanced. The vet can prescribe gistocal tablets to restore the calcium level. A broken front tooth will normally grow back, but you should check regularly that this is happening.

A rabbit's front teeth grow continuously and are ground down regularly by its gnawing. A genetic defect, a heavy blow or lack of gnawing opportunities can disrupt this process. Its teeth are ground irregularly and in the end don't fit together properly. In some cases the teeth continue to grow unchecked, even into the opposite jaw. When a rabbit's teeth are too long, it can no longer chew properly and the animal will lose weight and eventually starve to death.

Long teeth can easily be clipped back. A vet can show you how to do it.

Old age

Obviously we hope that your pet will grow old without disease and pain. However rabbits live nowhere near as long as humans and you must reckon with the fact that after just a few years you have an old rabbit to care for. Such an old rabbit will slowly become quieter and get grey hair in its coat, and now it needs a different kind of care. The time for wild games is over; it won't like them any more. Leave your rabbit in peace. In the last few weeks and days of its life, you will notice its fur decaying and the animal will get thinner. Don't try to force it to eat if it doesn't want to; the end is usually not long off. Rabbits, on average, live about five to seven years. In exceptional cases they can reach the age of fifteen.

Rabbit shull

Jaw abscess

Parasites

Parasites are small creatures that live at the cost of their host. The best known are fleas on dogs and cats. Rabbits seldom have problems with parasites, and certainly not healthy animals.

Flea

Weak, sick or poorly cared for animals, however, are far more likely to be affected. You mostly discover parasites only when an animal starts to scratch itself and gets bald patches. If you notice that your rabbit is itching and scratches itself frequently, then it's probably suffering from lice (tiny spiders that feed on blood). These lice are often spread by birds.

A pet shop or vet can advise you on dealing with parasites.

Fleas
There is a type of flea known as the rabbit flea, but the most common kind of flea found on rabbits are cat fleas. Rabbits are not especially vulnerable to them. If your other pets (especially cats and dogs) are free of fleas, then your rabbit will rarely have problems with them. But if your cat does suffer from fleas, then these will often make the jump to your rabbit. If you're treating a pet for fleas, then don't forget your rabbit(s). They are best treated with flea powder or spray. Make sure your rabbit cannot breathe it in.

Skin mites or mange
The skin mite is a particularly harmful parasite. Fortunately they seldom occur but if they do affect your rabbit, you've got work to do! The skin mite is a minute spider that creeps into its host's skin, making the mite itself almost never visible. It causes scabs and eczema, which can sometimes cover the whole skin within a month. Skin mites are infectious and can be passed on to other

animals. Your vet or a good pet shop will have treatments for skin mites. Read the instructions on the packaging thoroughly. In most cases the infected animal must be bathed in the substance. Dry your rabbit off well to prevent it catching a cold and put it in a warm place (minimum 25° C).

Worms

Ear mites

If your rabbit frequently shakes its head or holds it tilted, there's a good chance it's suffering from ear mites (or ear mange), which is also caused by tiny spiders. They feed on earwax and flakes of skin within the ear. The continuous irritation causes the ears to produce even more wax, which makes the whole ear fill with filth, causing heavy itching. You can diagnose ear mites by simply looking into the ear. Your vet can prescribe an ear cleaner, which will take care of them immediately.

Worms

A rabbit can also suffer from a number of internal parasites. These are tiny organisms that live inside its body, such as bandworm, ringworm and flukes. Worms and flukes are usually caught from dogs or wild rabbits, and are transferred by their droppings. If you pick grass for your rabbit in a place where dogs often run, or where wild rabbits live, this may hold this parasite's eggs. If your rabbit eats this grass, the eggs end up in its stomach. Here

they hatch and, slowly but surely, multiply. A rabbit with a worm infection may not become seriously ill straight away, but will lose weight and be more vulnerable to other diseases, so be careful where you pick grass for your pet.

Fungal skin infections

Rabbits can sometimes suffer from fungal skin infections, which leave tiny flakes of skin in their ears and nose. These infections are easily spread to other animals and humans, but they are easy to treat. Don't let such infections go on too long, because they can lead to all kinds of other problems. Your vet has good treatments for fungal infections.

Mite

Tips

- Beware of contagious diseases.
- Never buy animals in badly run shops.
- Take an excretion sample when you go to the vet's.
- Take rotting food out of the cage. It can cause illness.
- Choose good bedding. Sawdust often contains chemicals.
- Rabbits hate noise.
- Never let a rabbit nibble at house and garden plants.
- Offer your rabbit thistles and dandelion. It loves them!
- Never buy an animal that is too young.
- The importance of prevention not only applies to rabbits, but to all pets.
- Do not suddenly pull your hand back if your rabbit nibbles at it.
- Beware of insecticides. If in doubt, wash any fresh food.
- Draughts, damp, rotting or incorrect food, inadequate living space and overpopulation are factors which can affect your rabbit's health. Prevent them.
- Let your rabbit run free before feeding time. You can then lure it with a treat.
- Isolate a patient suffering from a contagious disease.
- Never feed your rabbit with sweets, cake or salty foods. It can become ill.
- Check the droppings when buying a rabbit.
- Never buy a rabbit on the spur of the moment.
- A rabbit is not a rodent.
- Make sure that food and water bowls cannot tip over.
- Put a paving slab into your rabbit's cage. This will help to keep its nails short.
- Visit a small animal show.
- Do not buy animals at an animal market.

Useful addresses

Rabbit Welfare Association
RWF, PO Box 603, Horsham,
West Sussex RH13 5WL.
National helpline - 01403 267658
http://www.houserabbit.co.uk/

**British Small Animal
Veterinary Association**
Woodrow House,
1 Telford Way, Waterwells
Business Park, Quedgeley,
Gloucester, GL2 2AB.
Telephone 01452 726700,
Administration Email:
adminoff@bsava.com
http://www.bsava.com

The R.R.E.C
The R.R.E.C exists to promote
kindness and understanding to
rabbits and rodents, whilst at the
same time, through their magazine,
Nibbling News, educating their
members on the care required by
the animals that so enrich their
lives.
The RREC PO Box 741,
Ampthill, MK45 1WZ
http://www.therrec.co.uk/

The BRC
This site has been designed for all
members and anyone who is inte-
rested in exhibiting rabbits as a
hobby or loves their pet rabbit.
info@thebrc.org
http://www.thebrc.org/

**The Rabbit Welfare
Project website**
Amongst other things, the Rabbit
Welfare Project aims to improve
rabbit welfare and knowledge,
and to re-home unwanted rabbits.
http://welcome.to/rabbitproject

The House Rabbit Society
The House Rabbit Society is an
all-volunteer, non-profit organisa-
tion situated in the USA that
rescues abandoned rabbits and
educates the public on rabbit care.
membership@rabbit.org
http://www.rabbit.org/

The rabbit on the Internet

The Internet is a useful source for information about rabbits. There is a wide range of websites and homepages dedicated to rabbits. From care to housing, history, pictures and health, almost anything can be found on the net. It is not difficult to find sites on the Internet. Type 'rabbit' into a search engine, and you will get a list with all the sites on offer. The list below names some of the sites. On each site, you will find many interesting links to other sites with information and news. Sometimes sites change their address and you can no longer find them. However, you can usually find them as a link on other sites. Enjoy surfing!

www.rabbitrehome.org.uk
At Rabbit Rehome UK rescue centres and individuals can enter details of rabbits in need of new homes and rabbit lovers can search for the rabbit that suits them best.

www.rabbitrehome.org.uk
At Rabbit Rehome UK rescue centres and individuals can enter details of rabbits in need of new homes and rabbit lovers can search for the rabbit that suits them best.

www.bunnymail.co.uk
Online-store. All you need for your rabbit on toys, grooming, accessories, foods and more.

http://homepage.mac.com/mattocks/ morfz/home.html
A website with lots of information on all topics related to rabbits. A great website.

www.carrotcafe.com
This website attempts to explain rabbit nutrition and feeding, not by telling you how to feed your bunny, but by telling you why you feed your bunny.

www.rabbitworld.com
Here you can find rabbit information on environment, diet, health and more.

www.bunnyheaven.co.uk
Another very informative website on rabbits, with lots of rabbit topics.

The Rabbit

Name:	Rabbit
Latin name:	*Oryctolagus cuniculus*
Origin:	Europe, now found worldwide
Length:	25-70 cm
Tail length:	3-6 cm
Ear length:	5 cm (Polish/coloured dwarf)
	up to 45 cm (French lop)
Weight:	800 grams (dwarf rabbit)
	- ca. 6-9 kg (Flemish Giant)
Body temperature:	37° C
Fertile age:	7 months
Ready to breed:	7 months
Pregnancy:	28-31 days
Number of young:	3-4 (max. 8)
Birth-weight:	45-70 grams
Eyes open:	after 10 days
Lactation:	6-8 weeks
Life expectancy:	5-7 years